The Christmas
STORY

*God's
Unspeakable
Gift*

As told by

PASTOR CHUCK SMITH

The Christmas Story
by Chuck Smith

© 2006 The Word For Today
Published by The Word For Today
P.O. Box 8000, Costa Mesa, CA 92628
(800) 272-WORD (9673)

Second Printing 2007

Web Site: www.twft.com
E-mail: info@twft.com

ISBN: 978-1-932941-91-3

Edited by Shannon Woodward
Interior design by Bob Bubnis

Printed in the United States of America

PREFACE

STORYTELLING IS A POWERFUL FORM OF communication. And no one knows that more than a pastor. Ask any pastor, and he'll tell you that when we look out over our congregation and we notice eyelids beginning to droop and heads beginning to bob, we know it's time to change direction. It's time for a story. "Once upon a time, many years ago . . ." we'll say. And lo and behold, people perk up. They start to listen. They tune in. That's because everyone loves a story. When you have their attention, you can use the subtlety of a story to convey important truths.

It saddens me that storytelling has so little part in our culture anymore. Instead of learning history and truth through stories passed down from grandparents, parents, aunts and uncles, children today get information from commercials, cartoons, movies, and video games. It's an uneven, empty trade, for the human touch is lost when storytelling is set aside.

But it needn't be so. It's never too late to gather your family and share a story together. And there's never a better time to begin again than at Christmas.

It is my desire that you might use this book to share the wonder of Christmas with your loved ones. An incredible thing happened in Bethlehem two thousand years ago. The birth of Jesus changed history forever. The Gift God sent that night opened prison doors, loosened shackles, and provided entry into heaven. It proved His love for mankind. Those who understand what happened that long ago night carry a bit of awe with them always. But the rest of the world remains ignorant and unseeing. The rest of the world has turned the celebration of the Christ Child into nothing more than a celebration of self.

No doubt, you will hear many carols during this holiday season. *"Hark! the Herald Angels Sing"* will play hundreds of times throughout malls and on radio stations in the month of December. But do people understand the tidings brought by those angels? Do they have any inkling whatsoever of the drama those angels spoke about?

"*Silent Night*" will play in the background at many parties in the coming weeks. That's a perennial favorite. But do people stop and ponder the incredible event that occurred on that quiet Bethlehem night?

You won't be able to step into a mall or department store without hearing "*Joy to the World.*" But think about it: do you have the joy that song sings about? Are you experiencing the joy of God's gift? Apart from Christ, the world does not understand or encounter that joy. A world bound and wrapped in sin cannot possibly experience true joy.

And yet the world tries. All around us, the world prepares itself to celebrate something they do not understand. Interspersed among the fat, bearded men in red, nativities are scattered, but most people have never grasped the glory of the manger. Among all the cards decorated with elves and holly and snowmen, an occasional silhouette of the wise men will appear, but most people have no idea what those men searched for. My neighborhood is gaily decorated with beautiful lights, but very few of my neighbors know the beauty of the true Light who came into the world. "He was in the world and the world was made by Him, but the world knew Him not." And the tragedy is that for the most part, this is still true today: the world knows Him not.

The Bible tells us that;

> ". . . faith cometh by hearing, and hearing by
> the word of God" (Romans 10:17).

It all begins with listening. The story between these covers is the answer to life's biggest question and greatest need. It tells of a love so deep, so immeasurable, and so unspeakable, that it must be heard with the heart. It describes a love so mysterious, the angels long to understand it; a love so powerful, it can create beauty from ashes, and breathe life into the dead. But how can we remember something we've never heard?

Each year as I read the Christmas story, the Holy Spirit kindles a different part of the story to life, revealing an exquisite beauty—the greatest love story ever told—God's love for us. I urge you to start a new tradition this year. Let the mound of presents remain a bit longer under the tree. They can wait. Instead of rushing to open trinkets that will rust and fade away with time, invite your family to turn their hearts toward the one Gift that will last for eternity. There's no better time to receive that Gift than on Christmas day.

There was born that night in Bethlehem a Savior, the Messiah, the Lord. God's gift of love for you. The most important gift of all. One that expresses a depth of love that we can never experience or understand.

I pray that this Christmas you'll open that package first. It will add joy and color and beauty to your day like you have never known before. In fact, you will really discover what Christmas is all about if you will receive God's Gift first.

"*And it came to pass,*" Luke's gospel begins. And with those words, God draws us in to His story. On a night darkened by hopelessness, hope came to earth . . .

And it came to pass in those days, that there went out a decree from Caesar Augustus that all the world should be taxed. (And this taxing was first made when Cyrenius was governor of Syria.) And all went to be taxed, every one into his own city. And Joseph also went up from Galilee, out of the city of Nazareth, into Judaea, unto the city of David, which is called Bethlehem; (because he was of the house and lineage of David:) to be taxed with Mary his espoused wife, being great with child. And so it was, that, while they were there, the days were accomplished that she should be delivered. And she brought forth her firstborn son, and wrapped him in swaddling clothes, and laid him in a manger; because there was no room for them in the inn.

—LUKE 2:1-7

Chapter 1
THE LIGHT

SHE WAS PROBABLY ONLY FIFTEEN OR SIXTEEN years old when she left her little village of Nazareth to make that long journey. Just a girl — a girl who was "great with child." But at a time when most mothers-to-be would be resting and staying close to their family and familiar surroundings, she left the safety of her home to obey the demands of a Roman emperor.

What thoughts do you suppose filled Mary's mind during that trip to Bethlehem? Did she think back on the moment she first heard that she would carry the Son of God in her womb? Maybe she replayed the angel's unexpected words, when she was told that she was blessed among all women, and that she'd found favor with God, and that He had chosen her to be the human instrument by which He would bring His Son into the world.

Mary couldn't understand at first. She asked, "How can this be, seeing that I am a virgin?" And the angel explained to her that the power of God would come upon her so that the Holy One that would be born of her would be known as the Son of God.

Some people say they have a problem with the virgin birth. The truth is, their problem really isn't with the virgin birth. Their problem is with their concept of God. After explaining to Mary how she would conceive God's Son, the angel reminded her, "With God nothing shall be impossible" (Luke 1:37). We would do well to remember that. We shouldn't have any problem with anything we read in Scripture, because with God, nothing is impossible. If you can believe the first verse of Genesis, which declares that God is the Creator of all things, then you shouldn't have a problem believing the rest of the Bible. You should understand that He's big enough and powerful enough to do whatever He says He's going to do.

Mary believed. She accepted the word of the angel, and then, in sweet surrender said,

> "Behold the handmaid of the Lord; be it unto me according to thy word" (Luke 1:38).

What a beautiful picture of submission.

Joseph, however, had a more difficult time accepting the news. Mary's startling announcement nearly ended their engagement.

Now, it's important to understand that back in those days, engagement was culturally different than it is today. Marriage back then was by arrangement. Maybe you're a five-year-old boy and your parents notice that some friends of theirs have a sweet, cute little daughter. They might get together and reach an agreement. "Why don't we arrange for our children to get married?" And so they would make the arrangements and you would be considered engaged. Just like that—even if you were only five. Can you imagine the first day of kindergarten, pointing across the room at that little girl and nudging your neighbor? "Guess what? I'm engaged to her."

It was a different world then, that's for sure. Engagements weren't made and broken like they are today. They were binding. One year before the actual wedding, the couple entered into a contract called "the espousal" in which they were totally committed to each other for this one-year period—even though the wedding had not yet taken place. If the groom-to-be should die in that year's time, the wife-to-be would be considered a widow. This was a contract of complete commitment to one another. To break this commitment, they would actually have to obtain a writ of divorce. It was during this year of espousal that the angel visited Mary and brought her the astounding news.

Joseph knew they'd remained pure, so the only thing he could conclude was that she'd been with another man during their espousal period. This put him in a quandary. If he reported her unfaithfulness publicly, the law demanded that she be stoned to death. Joseph didn't want that. He felt betrayed, but he also still loved Mary. So he was thinking about divorcing her quietly.

But God intervened. He sent an angel—this time to Joseph. The angel of the Lord spoke to Joseph in a dream and explained that the Child Mary carried had no earthly father. The angel said to him,

> "Joseph, son of David, do not be afraid to take to you Mary your wife, for that which is conceived in her is of the Holy Spirit. And she will bring forth a Son, and you shall call His name JESUS, for He will save His people from their sins" (Matthew 1:20-21 NKJV).

When he awoke, Joseph's fear had vanished. He took Mary as his wife, and watched as the Child within her grew. They would have stayed those final days in Nazareth — that small, insignificant village near the eastern edge of the Mediterranean Sea — quietly awaiting His birth, had it not been for a puffed up, power-hungry emperor named Caesar Augustus.

His given name wasn't Caesar. He'd been born Caius Octavianus. He adopted the name Caesar after his great-uncle, Julius Caesar. After gaining control as the first Roman emperor, he felt he needed a title. Someone suggested "king of Rome," but he vetoed that as being not quite important enough. Another suggested he go by the title of "dictator." But Caesar rejected that title as well. He said it sounded too temporary.

Finally, the newly formed Roman senate came up with the word "Augustus," which was a Latin word that meant "of the gods," suggesting a sort of divine appointment. Caesar liked the religious flavor of that title—and took it. And from that time on, it was generally accepted that the Roman Emperor was some kind of deity. Later, people would be forced to confess that Caesar was lord. But for the time being, Caesar contented himself with issuing demands and edicts.

No one disputed Caesar. No one dared. He held all the power, and he wasn't afraid to use it. He thought nothing at all about laying a heavy yoke upon the shoulders of his people—mainly in the form of taxation.

Also during this time, the gates to the temple of Janis, a pagan god, were closed. Janis was the Roman god of war, and whenever the Roman troops were engaged in battle, the gates to the temple of Janis would be opened and the people would go in and pray that Janis would give them victory over their enemies. At this present time in history, those gates had been closed ten years and would remain closed for another thirty years. You might think, "How wonderful! What a beautiful time for the Messiah, the Prince of Peace to be born!" But think again. Why was there peace? Because Caesar ruled the world with an iron fist. Under his rule, the Roman troops had smashed all resistance and so bludgeoned the world—the *whole world*—into submission that no man found the courage to speak up against them. No man dared call his soul his own. All were slaves to Rome. Instead of a beautiful time, this was one of the most horrific times in the history of the world.

So when Caesar thought that it would be nice to have more money, he issued a new tax on the world. No one thought to appeal or argue or resist. The decree went out: "All the world shall be taxed." According to the command, everyone was to go immediately to the town of their birth and register for the tax.

This is the reason we find Joseph and Mary on an eighty-mile journey to Bethlehem. Now, you might think, "That's not too bad. I make that kind of trip every day." But have you ever tried to walk it? We get in our air-conditioned cars and get on the freeway, and no, it isn't very far. But if you took that trip on foot, you would discover it is quite a distance—especially if you are pregnant and about ready to be delivered of your child.

I have to suppose that Joseph wasn't very happy as he led Mary along that arduous route from Nazareth to Bethlehem. He was a descendant of David. Royal blood coursed through his veins. His wife was about to give birth to the Son of God. No one in their right mind would make that kind of trip in those days under those conditions. Yet here they were, traveling at this critical time simply to satisfy the whim of a pompous little fellow in Rome.

I wonder if Joseph felt forsaken. I wonder if he cried out to God during that long journey to Bethlehem. "Where are You, Lord? Don't You see what is happening? Mary shouldn't be out here. She should be home, resting. . . ." Maybe he kicked at the rocks along the roadside, grumbling and thinking out loud, "Who is this man, Caesar, that I should have to obey him?"

It certainly looked, to human eyes, like Caesar was the one pulling the strings. After all, he had been the one to issue that ridiculous decree. The idea to send everyone scurrying back to their hometowns had been all his. Or had it?

There's always another side to the story. When the earthly details look bleak and small, it's good to remember the heavenly perspective.

Some seven hundred years before Joseph and Mary set out on their journey, the prophet Micah said,

> "And thou, Bethlehem, though thou be little among the provinces of Judah, yet out of thee shall come he who is to rule my people; whose goings forth have been of old, from everlasting" (Micah 5:2).

What was that? What did we read there? We read that Bethlehem—that little, insignificant village—had an important role to play in the fulfilling of prophecy. Of all the towns in all the world, God had chosen Bethlehem to be the birthplace of the Messiah. That changes the situation a bit, doesn't it? We realize, suddenly, that Caesar isn't the one pulling all the strings. He probably thought himself pretty clever to have come up with his money-grabbing scheme. He probably puffed out his chest as everybody bowed and submitted to his order. And yet Caesar was just a tool in God's hands. He was nothing more than God's puppet. God pulled the strings. He reached down, tapped Caesar on the shoulder and said, "I want you to order a taxation. Tell everyone to go to their hometowns and enroll for the tax." God used Caesar's greed to arrange the circumstances so that Joseph would help his bride up onto a donkey at the worst possible time in her pregnancy and move her eighty miles from the wrong town — Nazareth — to the right town — Bethlehem.

And so, late in her pregnancy and against all reason and logic and sound judgment, Mary made the perilous journey. I picture her resting her hand on her stomach as they crossed the distance, and wondering what awaited her in Bethlehem. The Child who lived in her womb would one day rule over the whole world in righteousness, justice, and peace. But first, He must be delivered. Would they find a proper place for His birth? Would they find a clean room; a quiet, private room?

If Mary entertained those hopes along her journey, they were dashed upon entering Bethlehem. The town swarmed with tax-enrolling visitors, all scrambling for a place to stay. Though Joseph tried, he could not find a suitable resting place for Mary.

When we read "there was no room for them in the inn," we picture the inns we're familiar with today. We think about walking up to the desk of a hotel, or motel, or bed and breakfast and renting a private room with a bed and a basin of water. Maybe waking to a nice continental breakfast in the lobby the next morning. But that's wrong. Inns back then were not the inns we have today. The word in the Greek is *katalumah*. It was an enclosure, plain and simple. Four walls; no ceiling. It was little more than a pen where people would enclose their animals and themselves for the night. So the best that Joseph and Mary could hope for was a pen where they might find shelter from the wind and wild animals. But even that was not to be. There was no room in the *katalumah.* Instead, they sought refuge in an area reserved for animals. Some say it was a stable; others say it was a cave. Either way, it was a place fit only for beasts.

And then . . . Mary went into labor. In a dark, smelly, unprotected cavern—with no midwife, no nurse, no female relatives or friends to assist her—this young girl delivered her child alone. Then she wrapped Him in swaddling clothes and laid Him in a manger. The Son of God—God's Gift to mankind—was laid in an animal trough.

Did He cry? We don't know. But if He did, it would have been appropriate. After all, the Child in that feeding trough had left the beauty of heaven to enter a world that would, in the end, despise and reject Him.

God controlled this event from the first detail to the last. And all of heaven, no doubt, watched the proceedings with great interest. It makes us wonder what God was thinking. Why would He allow His Son to enter the world in such a dismal, humble place? If I were God and sending my son into the world, I would make sure he was born in the finest hospital with the greatest doctors attending his entrance. I'd want to make sure that nothing went wrong. And if it couldn't be in a hospital, I'd arrange for the most luxurious room in the finest hotel. But God didn't choose an elegant place; not even a clean place. He arranged for His Son to enter the world in a home for animals, and provided only a trough for His first bed.

The Bible tells us;

> "He was in the world, and the world was made by him, and the world knew him not" (John 1:10).

Emmanuel — the King of kings and Lord of lords, the pre-existent One, the Creator — would come into a world that would not recognize or accept Him. He came in obscurity, in lowliness . . . on purpose. I think God planned for that common birth in that uncommon place so that the very least and poorest of us could identify with the Baby.

Not far from this birthplace, shepherds stood in a field keeping watch over their flocks. And in the midst of their ordinary evening, something extraordinary happened. An angel appeared . . . an angel with big news.

Before we follow the story any further, allow me a little speculation. Although this angel isn't named, I believe it was Gabriel. I think when we all get to heaven, you're going to find out I am right. You'll say, "Chuck said that."

I believe it was Gabriel for one simple reason: Gabriel had a hard time keeping secrets. Five hundred years before this event, Gabriel came to a prophet named Daniel, who was one of the captives in Babylon. While Daniel prayed and fasted, Gabriel appeared and gave him an understanding of the future. In fact, he told Daniel the exact time the Messiah would come. He told Daniel that from the time the commandment went forth to restore and rebuild Jerusalem until the coming of the Messiah, 483 years (or 69 seven-year cycles) would pass. That's pretty precise. Gabriel gave out the secret. He just couldn't help himself.

Five hundred years went by, and once again, Gabriel came visiting the earth. This time, he appeared to a priest named Zacharias who happened to be offering incense in the temple at the time. Gabriel had another secret to share. He told Zacharias that although he was an old man and his wife was an old woman, she was about to conceive a son, whom they were to call John. This child would go in the spirit and power of Elijah and be a forerunner of the Messiah. A short time later he appeared to Mary to inform her that she was highly favored by God, for God had chosen her to be the human instrument to bring His Son into the world.

That is why when I read that an angel appeared to the shepherds and proclaimed that the Messiah had been born, I can't help but think that the angel was Gabriel. I think that after overseeing the entrance of the Messiah into the world and making sure that He was safely swaddled, Gabriel had to find someone to share the news with. What else do you do with news this important? Nothing in all of history even came close in comparison with this event. Gabriel can't contain the news.

But he's got a problem. All of Bethlehem is asleep. The candles have all been blown out and the people are sleeping soundly. As Gabriel surveys the town, he notices the flicker of a fire off in the distance. He hastens over and finds a few shepherds watching their flocks at night.

Tradition suggests that these were actually temple shepherds watching the sheep that would be used for the daily temple sacrifices. We can't know for sure, but it's a beautiful idea. This special night as they are watching the sheep, all of a sudden there is a bright light, as the angel appears to inform them that the Light of the world, the Savior, the Messiah had just been born in Bethlehem. Suddenly the angel was joined by a multitude of heavenly host declaring, "Glory to God in the highest, peace on earth, good will toward men."

Through that Baby born in Bethlehem that night close to 2,000 years ago, peace with God is now possible. The question is, "Do you have that peace?"

"Glory to God in the highest, and on earth peace, good will toward men."

And there were in the same country shepherds abiding in the field, keeping watch over their flock by night. And, lo, the angel of the Lord came upon them, and the glory of the Lord shone round about them: and they were sore afraid.

LUKE 2:8-9

Chapter 2
THE DARKNESS

WHY WERE THE SHEPHERDS SO AFRAID? Granted, it would be startling to see a dark hillside suddenly lit up by heavenly light. But what exactly was it about the glory of the Lord shining upon them that caused those shepherds to tremble?

I think it's because that Light was unfamiliar to them. It was unfamiliar, and it stood in sharp contrast to everything they knew.

When you stop to think about it, it's really quite appropriate that the Messiah came at night. That's because when we think of nighttime, we think of darkness. We think of an absence of light. We think about stumbling around, groping, maybe tripping over things we cannot see. And that pretty well sums up the condition of the world on that long ago night. Those shepherds had never seen anything like the angel that stood before them. All they knew was darkness — they, and the rest of mankind.

The prophet Isaiah, in looking ahead to this very event, said,

> "The people that walked in darkness have seen a great light: they that dwell in the land of the shadow of death, upon them hath the light shined" (Isaiah 9:2).

It's interesting to take that passage and research the words in the original text. In the Hebrew, the word for "walked" is *halak,* which could be translated as "wandered." The word "darkness" is *choshek,* which could mean literal darkness, but it could also mean misery, destruction, death, ignorance, sorrow, or wickedness. The phrase "shadow of death," *tsalmaveth*, could be interpreted as "the grave." And aside from meaning "illumination," *owr,* the word for "light," could also mean "happiness."

So when you put those meanings together, you could translate Isaiah 9:2 as saying, *"The people that wandered in misery, ignorance and sorrow have seen a great light; they that dwell in the land of the grave, upon them hath happiness shined."*

Happiness shined on the miserable that night in Bethlehem. The Light came, and with His coming, darkness had no choice but to flee.

But why was the world so dark and miserable? To understand that, we have to go back to the garden.

When God placed Adam in the garden of Eden, He intended that the two of them would enjoy fellowship together. And for a time, it was so. Adam communed with God. The word "commune" is the same word that we use for "fellowship." Adam enjoyed fellowship with God. That was God's purpose in creating Adam. And God gave Adam an incredible home, a place of both beauty and blessing. Eden had everything Adam needed. He had been given all kinds of liberty and freedom and was commanded to just enjoy God's love and God's creation. There was only one restriction—one thing that God declared to be off limits. God took Adam on a little tour of the place, led him to the center of the garden, and stopped him in front of one particular tree. "Adam," He said, "you may eat freely of all the trees in this garden—with the exception of this one. You're not to eat of it. For in the day that you eat of this tree, you will surely die."

Eve, when she came along, knew also of the restriction. She knew what God had commanded. "Enjoy it all . . . but stay clear of that one particular tree."

We don't know exactly when Satan came to Eve, but I imagine he didn't wait too long. "Has God said that you can eat of all the trees that are in the garden?" he asked her.

Eve said, "Yes, with the exception of that one tree in the middle of the garden. God told us that if we would eat of it we would surely die."

Eve started well. She went right to the Word of God. But Satan disputed that Word. "You will not die," he lied. "God knows that in the day that you eat of that tree, you will become as God, knowing good from evil."

That snake.

Eve should have known better. She should have stepped back, considered the character of God, and said, "No. You're wrong. God doesn't lie." Instead, she let the liar draw her in. She let him change her perception of God. In his cunning way—and we know from Genesis 3:1 that;

> "the serpent was more cunning than any beast
> of the field which the LORD God had made."

Satan used those lies to systematically destroy Eve's confidence in the Lord. "God's trying to hold you back, Eve. He's keeping something good and beneficial from you. How unfair! And you know why He's doing that, Eve? He's doing it to protect Himself. He's afraid of you becoming as He is."

That liar.

Eve bought his lie. She fell right into his trap. Ignoring what she knew of God, she reached her hand out, snatched the forbidden fruit, and took a bite. Then she turned to Adam and urged him to do the same. Eve may have been deceived, but Adam was not. Scripture makes this fact clear. Paul tells us in 1 Timothy 2:14,

> "And Adam was not deceived, but the woman being deceived was in the transgression."

Adam accepted that fruit and took a bite knowing full well that he was disobeying God.

The bite did bring death. Though physically, Adam and Eve continued breathing and blinking and walking around; spiritually, they died. Their fellowship with God was broken — and self-awareness was born.

You see, up until this time, Adam and Eve had lived in a God-conscious state. But the result of their sin brought them into a self-conscious state. We read in Genesis 3:7,

> "And the eyes of them both were opened, and they knew that they were naked; and they sewed fig leaves together and made themselves aprons."

They hadn't had this awareness before . . . but now they knew.

And then we read something heartbreaking. We read that God came into the garden looking for them. He wanted communion with His children. He wanted fellowship with them. But for the first time ever, they didn't come running at the sound of His voice. They didn't come eagerly to meet Him. Instead, they hid themselves.

> "And they heard the voice of the LORD God walking in the garden in the cool of the day: and Adam and his wife hid themselves from the presence of the LORD God amongst the trees of the garden" (Genesis 3:8).

Sin brings heartbreaking consequences. It brings spiritual death, self-consciousness, and shame. It drives a wedge between God and His children. Adam—who had once lived on a spiritual level, communing with the God of all creation—had now lowered himself to living on a purely physical level. His mind, which had once been filled with thoughts of God, was now completely absorbed with his bodily needs.

Satan got his way. He used his lies to destroy the relationship between God and His children. When Adam sinned, and his spirit died and he lost fellowship with God, he entered into a purposeless existence—as did all who came after Adam.

But God made another way for that communion to take place. In the Law, God laid down rules for living whereby fellowship could be restored. He gave certain commandments, which, if kept, would allow men to continue fellowshiping with Him. But God knew men would not always keep those commandments. So He made provision for that, too. He said, "If you fail to keep these commandments, you can restore our fellowship by sacrificing an animal. You can lay your hands upon the head of that animal and transfer your guilt to that animal. When it dies, and its blood flows over the altar, your sins will be atoned for—and our fellowship will be restored."

Through the establishment of the sacrificial system, God revealed something sobering about sin: sin brings death. Death is the payment for sin. Innocent blood must be shed to cover the consequences of sin.

Because God desires intimacy and fellowship with His children—and because He knew that in order for us to have fellowship with Him, we must first know Him—God continued to find ways to reveal Himself. He revealed Himself to man in nature. In Psalm 19:1-3 we read,

> "The heavens declare the glory of God; and
> the firmament sheweth his handywork.

Day unto day uttereth speech, and night unto night sheweth knowledge. There is no speech nor language, where their voice is not heard."

In the vastness of the universe, we saw the vastness of God. In the intricacies of minute life forms, we saw the infinite wisdom and creativity of God. Nature speaks a universal language that can be understood by every man, so that every man has an opportunity to grasp the existence of God.

Nature tells us God exists, but it doesn't give a defined, clear message about God's character. Thus, men began to invent their own concepts of who God was. In order to correct those misconceptions, God began to reveal Himself to men through another means. We read in Hebrews 1:1 that God, "at various times and in various ways spoke in time past to the fathers by the prophets."

God first revealed Himself to Noah, showing Himself to be righteous and holy. God told Noah that the world must be judged because they had forsaken Him and His ways. When God brought condemnation upon that corrupt, unbelieving world, Noah saw not only God's righteousness, but also His justice.

Next, God revealed Himself to Abraham. When Abraham heard God's voice, he responded by leaving his homeland, even though he didn't know where God was taking him. God called him out of Babylon, the seat of false world religions. He called Abraham to be apart from the world so that they could commune together. And God promised Abraham not only land, but also descendants—descendants from which would come the Messiah.

Through the revelation God gave Moses, we began to understand the rules that we must follow if we are to live in fellowship with God. And from Moses, continuing on through the remainder of the Old Testament, God revealed Himself further through prophets who cried out to the people, warning them that if they failed to keep God's rules, the judgment of God would fall.

God did all that so that men would know Him and reach for Him. But it seemed that the more God revealed Himself, the farther away men wandered. God's people kept moving farther and farther away from God, until finally they were so far away that it became necessary for God to cut them off completely. As God said through Jeremiah the prophet,

> "My people have committed two evils; they have forsaken me the fountain of living waters, and hewed them out cisterns, broken cisterns, that can hold no water" (Jeremiah 2:13).

Man's concepts of God became garbled and confused. They became corrupted. Because they saw the judgment of God upon the land, they began to think of God in terms only of judgment. They looked on Him as a fierce judge, a harsh lawgiver. They thought that in His anger, God looked upon them with condemnation. They got the wrong idea. And those wrong perceptions caused men to feel estranged and far from God.

Just like he did with Eve, Satan has worked on men's perceptions all through the centuries, trying to put distance between God and His children. Satan is a liar from the beginning. The truth is nothing to our enemy. He can swear to tell the truth, the whole truth, and nothing but the truth and just turn right around and lie. His deception and his lies have led countless people into bondage and into corruption. To Satan the truth is anything that promotes his cause, and his cause is to destroy you. Thus, he constantly contradicts the Word of God, even as he did with Eve. He will use any means to make you think God is against you, and not for you.

I have been accused of being a doting grandfather. And I must confess, the accusations are correct. I am guilty as charged. I love to dote on my grandchildren. Their parents—my children—tell me they have an extremely difficult time handling their children for a few days after they have been with Grandpa. Maybe that's because my grandchildren can do no wrong in my eyes. To me, their temper tantrums are just cute little ways of expressing their frustrations.

Now, that doesn't mean that I am not stern at times with my grandchildren. At times I have to say no to my grandkids. Those little master psychologists will do their best to make you feel guilty when they want something. When they don't get what they want, they'll say, "I knew you didn't love me." Oftentimes I'll say, "Because I love you I'm not getting it for you. You don't need that .22 rifle."

And sometimes I have to correct them. I have one little grandson who is especially rambunctious. He's a great little guy. He's just energetic. Many times when we pull into the parking lot of the toy store, he gets out of the car and starts running. He's so anxious to get in that store so Grandpa can buy him a toy. When he starts running through the parking lot, I have to call his name sharply. "Stop!" I say. "Don't you ever run through the parking lot. Let Grandpa hold your hand and you walk with Grandpa, because it's dangerous to run through the parking lot." I say it very sternly and very severely. I'm not mad at my grandson. I'm concerned for his safety. And he knows that. He'll look up at me with that smile of his and say, "Sorry, Gramps." And all is forgiven and we go in and get the toy.

God is a Father who loves to dote on His children. But sometimes, when we do things that are dangerous or even life-threatening, God has to pull us up short. He has to speak sternly. And what does Satan do? He comes up to us and says, "See how God hates you? He doesn't love you at all, or He wouldn't be so mean."

In reality, God is protecting you. He sees the danger you're about to walk into. Because He loves you, He sometimes has to deal with you firmly. Contrary to Satan's lies, that's not a sign of the absence of God's love — it's proof of God's love. The Bible speaks of God's correction, and tells us what our response should be.

> "Do not despise the chastening of the LORD, nor be discouraged when you are rebuked by Him; for whom the LORD loves He chastens, and scourges every son whom He receives" (Hebrews 12:5-6 NKJV).

Sometimes the Father finds it necessary to chasten us for love's sake — but how quickly we misinterpret that. How quick we are to forget God's character, ignore His voice, and listen instead to Satan's lies. Though God's Word says that God loves you, Satan says, "How can God love you? Look at what a mess you've made of your life." God's Word says, "There is therefore now no condemnation to them which are in Christ Jesus" (Romans 8:1), but Satan says, "God is sick and tired of dealing with your weaknesses and your failures. You're out." Yet God's Word says that;

"If we confess our sins, He is faithful and just to forgive us our sins, and to cleanse us from all unrighteousness" (1 John 1:9).

But Satan says, "Your sins are too great. God can't possibly forgive you."

That one act of disobedience there in the garden has affected us all. One moment of willfulness—one single bite—brought suffering on all generations throughout all of history. The Bible tells us;

> ". . . through one man sin entered the world, and death through sin, and thus death spread to all men . . ." (Romans 5:12 NKJV).

Adam's fall brought pain, isolation, frustration, shame, guilt, and hopelessness. In all times and in all places, men have suffered the consequences of Adam's sin.

God saw. He saw the suffering, the sorrow, the pain that sin had brought into our world. And God saw that there were some men who longed to be free from the power and slavery of sin, who longed and struggled and desired a better life. When nature was not enough to reveal His heart, when the Law proved powerless to move men closer to Him, when the voices of the prophets were not loud enough to break through our consciences, God found another way to speak to us and reveal His great love for mankind.

He sent a Child that night in Bethlehem. But the one He sent was not just any child — it was God's own Son, who would stand in our place, take our punishment, and pay for our sins.

We're all aware of our need for cleansing. We each know the depth of our own sins. The shepherds on that hillside knew the anguish of their sins. What they didn't yet know, in that moment when the glory of heaven shone around them and their knees locked in fright, was that their salvation had finally come. They didn't yet know that Hope had just drawn breath in a nearby stable, and that God had sent a Light to pierce their darkness.

The tidings brought by that angel were great indeed. In fact, the message would change history itself.

"For unto us a child is born, unto us a son is given: and the government shall be upon his shoulder: and his name shall be called Wonderful, Counsellor, The mighty God, The everlasting Father, The Prince of Peace."

—Isaiah 9:6

And the angel said unto them, Fear not: for, behold, I bring you good tidings of great joy, which shall be to all people. For unto you is born this day in the city of David a Saviour, which is Christ the Lord. And this shall be a sign unto you; Ye shall find the babe wrapped in swaddling clothes, lying in a manger. And suddenly there was with the angel a multitude of the heavenly host praising God, and saying, Glory to God in the highest, and on earth peace, good will toward men.

—LUKE 2:10-14

Chapter 3
THE GIFT

 ${ }^{}$ T'S HARD TO BE PATIENT WHEN YOU'RE waiting for something wonderful, isn't it? Those shepherds had been waiting a long time. And not just they, but the whole Jewish race had been waiting and longing for and anticipating the news that angel brought. They had prayed for this day — the day when the Messiah would come and bring them back into God's favor and into His divine purpose and ideal. Throughout the centuries, they had looked toward the time when the kingdom of God would come upon the earth.

And now the Savior had come at last. The promised Messiah had finally made His appearance.

I wonder if any of those shepherds experienced a moment of doubt when they heard the glorious news. Did they accept it wholeheartedly, or did a skeptic or two lurk among that small gathering of startled men? If any did harbor doubts or entertain any skeptical thoughts, those doubts would likely have scattered by the time the heavenly host joined that first angel and began lifting their voices in praise. How could doubt live in the presence of all that worship?

The multitude of angels was probably enough to convince the hesitant few that their long-awaited Messiah had indeed come. But if that wasn't enough, the weight of prophecy could easily back up the angel's announcement. If the shepherds needed proof, all they had to do was to look to Scripture.

God, you see, made it very easy for us. When He devised the plan to send His Son into the world to take our sins and die in our place, God gave to men many signs whereby His Son could be recognized. Within the pages of His Word, He wove a vivid description of His Son and planted evidence that would be indisputable when looked at in the light of His coming.

A lot of people over the ages have come along and claimed that they were the savior of the world. Those people were all loony tunes or else they were purposefully lying, but either way, they usually managed somehow to gather a following of gullible souls. More false leaders will undoubtedly come along. Scripture warns us of this. In Matthew 24:24-25 (NKJV), Jesus said,

> "False christs and false prophets will rise and show great signs and wonders to deceive, if possible, even the elect. See, I have told you beforehand."

Isn't God good? The warning is right there, right in the words of Scripture — and yet people continue to believe the false claims of these false messiahs. With just a little research through the Bible, you could easily dispute those claims. All you have to do is look at the signs God gave whereby His Son could be recognized.

For starters, we're told the Messiah would have to come through a specific lineage. He would have to be a descendant of Abraham, Isaac, Jacob, Jesse and David.

In Genesis 12:3, God told Abraham,

". . . in thee shall all families of the earth be
blessed."

After Ishmael (whom he had with Hagar) and
Isaac (whom he conceived with Sarah), Abraham
went on to have six more sons through his con-
cubine, Keturah. So of those eight sons, how do
we know which son was to carry the blessing to
all the families of the earth? We know because
God got more specific with Abraham. He went
on, a few chapters later, to clarify that this blessing would come through Isaac.

"And God said, Sarah thy wife shall bear thee
a son indeed; and thou shalt call his name
Isaac: and I will establish my covenant with
him for an everlasting covenant, and with his
seed after him" (Genesis 17:19).

And then, because Isaac had two sons — Esau and Jacob — and God wanted to make sure there was no misunderstanding about which son the blessing would come through, God further refined His prophecy. To Isaac himself, God said,

> "Dwell in this land, and I will be with you and bless you; for to you and your descendants I give all these lands, and I will perform the oath which I swore to Abraham your father. And I will make your descendants multiply as the stars of heaven; I will give to your descendants all these lands; and in your seed all the nations of the earth shall be blessed; because Abraham obeyed My voice and kept My charge, My commandments, My statutes, and My laws" (Genesis 26:3-5 NKJV).

God also confirmed this prophecy through Balaam who said,

"I see Him, but not now; I behold Him, but not near; a Star shall come out of Jacob; a Scepter shall rise out of Israel, and batter the brow of Moab, and destroy all the sons of tumult" (Numbers 24:17 NKJV).

The prophecies pick up again ten generations later with Jesse, a descendant of Jacob.

"And in that day there shall be a Root of Jesse, who shall stand as a banner to the people; for the Gentiles shall seek Him, and His resting place shall be glorious" (Isaiah 11:10 NKJV).

After Jesse comes David.

"Behold, the days are coming," says the LORD, "that I will raise to David a Branch of righteousness; a King shall reign and prosper, and execute judgment and righteousness in the earth. In His days Judah will be saved, and Israel will dwell safely; now this is His name by which He will be called: THE LORD OUR RIGHTEOUSNESS" (Jeremiah 23:5-6 NKJV).

The question is, did the Baby in the manger come from this particular line? Did Jesus descend from the line of David—from Abraham, Isaac and Jacob? Yes. Luke in his gospel traces the lineage of Mary through David, Jesse, Jacob, and Isaac to Abraham.

How many "messiahs" do you know who can claim the same?

God gave other signs, specific evidence, so that men could know that the true Messiah had come. He would need to be born of a virgin. Isaiah foretold it plainly:

"Therefore the Lord himself shall give you a sign; Behold, a virgin shall conceive, and

bear a son, and shall call his name Immanuel"
(Isaiah 7:14).

In addition, this birth was to take place in
Bethlehem.

"But thou, Bethlehem Ephratah, though thou
be little among the thousands of Judah, yet out
of thee shall he come forth unto me that is to
be ruler in Israel; whose goings forth have been
from of old, from everlasting" (Micah 5:2).

Mary—who had known no man—laid her
newborn Son in a manger in Bethlehem. In his
matter-of-fact way, Luke spells out all the details
for us.

"And Joseph also went up from Galilee, out
of the city of Nazareth, into Judaea, unto the
city of David, which is called Bethlehem;
(because he was of the house and lineage of

David:) to be taxed with Mary his espoused wife, being great with child. And so it was, that, while they were there, the days were accomplished that she should be delivered. And she brought forth her firstborn son, and wrapped him in swaddling clothes, and laid him in a manger; because there was no room for them in the inn" (Luke 2:4-7).

How many self-proclaimed "messiahs" came from virgin mothers? How many can prove they were born in Bethlehem?

The Gift wrapped in swaddling clothes would grow to be a man who would ride a donkey into Jerusalem precisely 483 years after the commandment was given to restore and rebuild Jerusalem from the Babylonian destruction—just as prophecy in Daniel said He would. He would be despised and rejected, betrayed by a friend for thirty pieces of silver, and crucified with transgressors. And then, three days after His death, He would rise again.

Now, do you know anyone else in history who met these interesting qualifications? Someone who came along in 32 AD riding on a donkey, who was later betrayed by a friend, crucified between thieves, but yet rose again on the third day? You don't. It's not possible. Jesus alone fulfilled these specific acts of proof. In His coming, in His birth, in His life, in His death and resurrection, Jesus fulfilled over 300 prophecies from the Old Testament, proving beyond a shadow of doubt that He is the promised Messiah; that He is everything that God said the Messiah would be.

The news shared on that quiet hillside was great indeed. Truly, it was "tidings of great joy."

The Gift in the manger was the answer to man's greatest need. As God had promised and foretold in the Scriptures, Emmanuel had come. In the Hebrew, that word *Emmanuel* means "with us is God." God with us. He had promised that one day He would come and dwell with man—and that day had arrived.

It's always nice when you get a gift that you need, instead of something you don't. God is a wonderful gift-giver. He knows just what we need. He looked over humanity and saw everything man had tried to do to fix his own sin problem, and then He sent the perfect solution—the one true Gift that had the power to solve man's problem once and for all.

By the time Jesus—*Emmanuel*—came to earth, mankind had already tried numerous things to bring satisfaction and joy and freedom from the bondage of sin. And we've been trying ever since. We've tried letting our flesh rule over us, but all that caused was strife — constant struggling, constant wars. We've tried various forms of government, hoping to somehow achieve a utopia on earth. But every form of government has failed, because governments are made up of people. When you have people at the helm, you have greed at the helm. And greed brings nothing but corruption.

Eventually, philosophers came along and began searching for the reason and purpose of our existence. They thought that by harnessing all their brainpower, they might possibly hit on an idea for how mankind might experience joy and achieve a sense of well-being and purpose.

They thought their ideas might bring the peace men hungered for. Philosophy used to search for beauty and truth, but when that search kept yielding nothing but emptiness—causing mankind to despair—philosophy itself eventually despaired. So the Greeks concluded in their philosophic system that man could not be saved, because that which is corrupt will always be corrupt. They determined that there is no salvation for mankind.

Philosophy today has continued its miserable course. Philosophy today believes there is no universal truth, no good. Instead, beauty and truth are "relative." If you think something to be beautiful, then it's beautiful. If you think something to be good, or true, or honorable, or acceptable, then that thing is as you believe. Just as in the days of the judges, mankind continues to do whatever is right in their own eyes. And that plan has brought nothing but heartache.

After philosophy proved to be no help, reformers came along and tried to fix the problem of sin and despair—men and women who tried fervently to reform the world in which we live. But that was a futile hope. You can't reform society. All you do is rearrange all the old, corrupt pieces. What you end up with is a new picture out of the old puzzle—and it's just as ugly. You succeed in doing nothing but putting a new ribbon on the old box. Prettying up the outside doesn't change the contents one bit.

No, the world was not in need of another philosopher. It didn't need another politician. It didn't need another reformer. What we needed was a Transformer. And so God sent His Son to transform the world.

Throughout history, philosophers and religious figureheads have been pretty free with their advice and their judgment. "Here's what you must do to change," they say. But they offer no help in changing. Buddha said, "This is the way you ought to live," and he pointed to a path. But he gave mankind no power, no capacity to walk in that path. All he brought was more frustration. Confucius said, "I know the secret. This is how man ought to live," and again pointed to a path but he didn't provide the power to walk that path either. Only Jesus provides both the guidance and the power to transform a life. "This is the way you should live," He says, "but you can't live that way in your own power. Take My hand and I'll give you the strength to follow the path. Open the door and let Me come into your life and I will dwell within you. I'll provide everything you need to live the life God meant for you to live."

The Child born that long ago night was not just a spouter of philosophies. He wasn't a reformer. He wasn't just another religious man; nor was He merely a prophet or a judge. The Child born to us that night is God's Son, the Savior of the world. He came to refute the lies of the enemy and reveal the lovingkindness of the Father to a world of fatherless orphans. He came to provide a way of escape for those chained to sin. He came to take the sting out of death; to rob the grave of its victory.

And He came to bring peace. He came to end the war between God and man; to rectify Adam's sin, bring mankind back to the garden, and restore the relationship we were meant to have with our Creator.

As the saying goes, "Good things come in small packages." On that dark night in Bethlehem, the saying was proved to be true. Within that rough, dirty manger, wrapped in a tiny, nondescript bundle, was the most incredible gift the world has ever received. In that one small Child, God had sent the answer to man's every need.

He sent us an Advocate (1 John 2:1), that we would know we weren't alone.

He sent the Bread of Life (John 6:35), that we would never again know hunger.

He sent the Living Water (John 4:10), that we would never thirst again.

He sent the Prince of Peace (Isaiah 9:6), that we could rest from our wars.

He sent the Counsellor (Isaiah 9:6), that we would gain wisdom and guidance.

He sent the Everlasting Father (Isaiah 9:6), that we would know eternal love.

He sent the Good Shepherd (John 10:11), that we would have a protector.

He sent the Light of the world (John 8:12), that we would never again stumble.

He sent the Deliverer (Romans 11:26), that our bondage would end.

He sent the great High Priest (Hebrews 4:14), that we could approach God.

He sent us Hope (1 Timothy 1:1), that our despair would finally end.

He sent Truth (John 14:6), that our blind eyes would be opened.

He sent us a Lamb (Revelation 13:8), that our sins could be covered.

He sent a Lion (Revelation 5:5), that we would be victorious.

He sent a Saviour (2 Timothy 1:10), that death would be abolished forever.

It's no wonder the angels lifted their voices and worshiped on that quiet hillside. The Father had sent the world an expression of His love. Light had pierced the world's darkness. The Child had arrived.

All that remained was a question: who — among the lost, the lonely, the broken, the hungry, the needy, and the captive — would reach out their hands and receive God's gift?

And it came to pass, as the angels were gone away from them into heaven, the shepherds said one to another, Let us now go even unto Bethlehem, and see this thing which is come to pass, which the Lord hath made known unto us. And they came with haste, and found Mary, and Joseph, and the babe lying in a manger. And when they had seen it, they made known abroad the saying which was told them concerning this child. And all they that heard it wondered at those things which were told them by the shepherds. But Mary kept all these things, and pondered them in her heart. And the shepherds returned, glorifying and praising God for all the things that they had heard and seen, as it was told unto them.

—LUKE 2:15-20

Chapter 4
THE CHOICE

"And they came with haste," Luke tells us. Apparently, the shepherds got over their fright. Somehow, the wondrous news fought its way past their terror and into their hearts. Their knees quit knocking. They believed. And they "came with haste" to Bethlehem to see the Child sent by God.

We read further that they came with haste and they saw that little Baby wrapped in swaddling clothes lying there. I am certain that they could not conceive, nor fully understand, all the mysteries of that evening—the infinite mysteries of the grace and love of God that was to be revealed in this Child. In fact, here we are with the advantage of 2,000 years of hindsight as we look upon that same scene, and we still stand with open-mouthed awe not fully understanding all of the infinite grace of God in the Child that was born that night. But with our last view of the shepherds as they left the manger and disappeared over the distant hillside, we read that they returned glorifying and praising God. Though they didn't fully comprehend or understand the full depth of the Gift in the manger, one look at Him had filled their hearts with praise. With their own eyes, they had beheld the unspeakable love of God.

It might not have turned out so. When the angels appeared on that hillside, the shepherds faced a choice. They could have ignored the glad tidings of the angel. They could have waited politely for the heavenly host to finish their praise and worship, waved good-bye to their nighttime visitors, and gone back to sheep-tending . . . unmoved, unchanged. But they made a better choice. They chose to receive God's Gift.

Have you ever tried to give someone a gift that they refused? Imagine how frustrating that would be. Imagine that you're a husband, and you've decided you want to demonstrate to your wife just how much you love her. So for Christmas, you head out shopping and look all day long until you find the exact right gift for her—something so perfect, so costly, that she won't be able to help but realize how great your love is for her. It doesn't matter that when you find what you're looking for, you put down every cent you own on the gift. You don't even blink as you sign a contract declaring that you're willing to make payments for the next five years on the remaining amount. The payments themselves will be incredibly difficult to make. You'll make those payments, but it's going to stretch your budget to the very limit. And yet you don't mind a bit. That's how determined you are to prove your love for your wife. She's so important to you that as far as you're concerned, no sacrifice is too great.

So you've got the gift. It's perfect. You even pay extra for beautiful gift-wrapping and a big bow. When you return home and walk into the house, you bend down and brush a few pine needles out of the way, then arrange the gift under the tree at just the right angle, so that she'll be able to see it when she comes into the room.

You can't wait for Christmas. You count the days until she can take the wrapping off and see what you did for her. And then, finally, the big day arrives. It's Christmas morning! You wake with a smile, knowing that this is the day when she'll realize just how much she means to you.

You almost can't taste your breakfast. The excitement is too great. But you get through it, and then you and your wife go into the living room together. Finally, the moment has arrived. She starts attacking the pile of packages you've placed under the tree. One by one, your wife opens each with surprise. She's so delighted with the little trinkets and knickknacks you've given her, you can hardly wait to see the expression on her face when she gets to the costliest gift. Three gifts are left . . . then two . . . then that one remaining gift. . . .

But wait! She's getting up. She's walking out of the room. What's going on?

"Time to get lunch started," she says over her shoulder as she walks into the kitchen.

"Hold on!" you argue. "Aren't you forgetting something? There's still one more package under that tree!"

She pops her head around the doorway. "Oh, yes . . . hmm. Well, maybe I'll open that one someday."

That's not going to do. "How about you open it right now?" you suggest.

She shakes her head. "No, I've opened all I want for now. Maybe another time." And she's off to tend to lunch.

Your love is in that package. All your expressions of affection wait under that wrapping. And you just know that as soon as the bow is set aside and the paper discarded, the one you love is going to understand what she means to you.

But she refuses to open that gift. All during this long day, you wait for your wife to return to the tree and finally take that package in hand. But she doesn't. When the two of you turn in for bed that night, your gift is still lying unopened under the tree. And the same thing happens the next day. A week goes by. Two weeks. Then months . . . and then years. The package is now sitting in a corner—dusty, unopened, unused, ignored. All of your sacrifice, all of your love goes unappreciated and rejected. The joy you expected has turned into nothing but disappointment.

Have I broken your heart yet? I hope so. Because that's a picture of what happens whenever one of

God's children refuses to accept the Gift He sent on that quiet Bethlehem night. The expression of His love dwells in the Christ Child, and yet for many, the Gift remains unopened and unaccepted. How disappointed God must be, after making such a great and meaningful sacrifice.

The ironic thing is that those same people love to celebrate Christ's birth. They get all excited over the trinkets they receive at Christmas. So much joy, so much laughter, so many expressions of love. And yet one gift remains unopened — the most important gift; the one that expresses an unspeakable love. God's love goes begging, while people sing carols and drink eggnog and swap junk.

And yet He waits. He waits for His children to choose Him.

Among the items exchanged this Christmas, you can be sure a number of Barbies will be in the mix. Elmo, too. He's always a hot item. Within days of the new Elmo doll first hitting the market, the threat of violence erupted between shoppers in department stores. It's crazy. I don't care how cute a little giggling red toy is, you'd never see me getting violent over it.

The truth is, you'd be hard pressed trying to develop a meaningful relationship with Barbie or Elmo. It's not going to happen. There's only so much enjoyment you can derive from a pre-programmed, mechanical toy—even one that talks.

I'll tell you who is not too interested in Barbie and Elmo, and that's God. He could have filled the world with mechanical objects, all designed to obey whatever He said and respond like clockwork and offer nice expressions of praise with the pull of a string. God could have made man to be nothing more than a talking robot, and He would have saved Himself a lot of grief. But He didn't do that. He knew that a mechanical relationship is a meaningless relationship. So God gave to us the capacity of choice. We can choose to fellowship with God or we can choose not to fellowship with God, but the choice is ours to make. It's the only way God could ensure that the relationships He does have are meaningful. How could you possibly enjoy a relationship you have with someone who was forced to be in that relationship? You couldn't.

But for the choice to be valid, God had to provide an alternate choice — and it had to be something attractive. So along with all of the good fruit-bearing trees that God placed in the garden, He put one more delicious-looking tree there among the rest. Despite its attraction, God warned man not to eat of the fruit of that tree. And thus the choice was presented. Would Adam obey, or would he rebel? Would Adam take God at His Word, or would he question his Maker?

We know how that turned out. Unfortunately, Adam made the wrong choice. He chose foolishly, and brought the curse of sin into the world. And in that moment, the death process began.

When man's fellowship with God was lost, a void was created. Within man, there is still something that yearns for a relationship with God. We long to fill that void but instead of turning to the only solution, we instead try to fill the void with false gods and the worship of things.

This Christmas season, many people will be on a search for fulfillment. They fool themselves into thinking that if they create just the right holiday atmosphere, they might bring permanent happiness into their homes. They convince themselves that if they buy (or receive) the perfect gifts, they might somehow chase the emptiness they live with all the rest of the year. But those hopes are foolish and futile. Maybe for a few days, or even a few weeks, they might feel a measure of satisfaction or happiness. But gradually, that false joy wears off, leaving only a hunger and a thirst for a meaningful relationship with God. That's because no matter how hard you try, you can't put a square peg in a round hole. God belongs in that empty place in the heart of man. No "thing" can take His place.

My question for you today is this: which kind of celebrator are you? Are you one who gets so caught up in the outward wrappings of Christmas — the noise, the lights, the extra strain and financial pressure, the crass commercialism, crowds, and chaos — that you forget the real meaning behind Christmas? Or are you one who understands, one who heard the glad tidings of the Christmas message and held your hands out to receive the Christ Child and all He brings?

Only two readers will pick up this book: those who are still searching, and those whose hunger has been satisfied. Those who still carry the burden of their guilt and condemnation, and those who have known the lightness and freedom of forgiveness. My prayer is that if you're the first kind, you'll realize the opportunity you've been given. You won't keep a safe distance from the manger this year. Instead, you'll draw closer and look intently at the Baby inside. You'll let God open your eyes to the truth — that He's the answer to every need you have, every longing.

God loves you and He wants to bless you. He wants to give you a life that is abundant and satisfying. You won't find the kind of life He offers by following the world's example. The world wants you to believe that you can find satisfaction in things, but that's wrong.

I read a story once about a couple of gravediggers who were ordered to dig an unusually large hole for an upcoming funeral. As they dug this large hole, they wondered together, "What in the world? This hole is huge! How big is this person who is going to be buried?"

The two men were so curious, they lurked around the gravesite once it was finished just waiting for the hearse to pull up so they could see who was being buried. But no hearse came. Instead, a pink Cadillac drove up.

Inside that pink Cadillac, a woman was strapped to the front seat. It turns out she was a very wealthy woman who had instructed, in her will, that several adjoining gravesites be bought so that she could be buried in her beloved pink Cadillac.

As the crane was carefully positioning the Cadillac down into the enormous hole, one of the gravediggers turned to the other and said, "Now, that's real living."

No. That's not real living. Many people have bought into the Madison Avenue philosophy, which would have you to think that "real living" is having good breath and pearly white teeth. It's a fishing trip with the boys up in the Rockies, or it's a wild party with a bunch of loose women. Or it's a nice home, a tough truck, or a fancy car — a car so nice you'd like to be buried in it.

The world is confused as to what real life is all about. They just don't understand real living. They haven't figured out that physical living is not the same thing as spiritual living, nor do they understand the wealth that is available to them through Christ.

Do you realize all that Jesus came to bring you? He said, contrasting the abundant life He brings with the destruction the enemy brings,

> "All that ever came before me are thieves and robbers: but the sheep did not hear them. I

am the door: by me if any man enter in, he shall be saved, and shall go in and out, and find pasture. The thief cometh not, but for to steal, and to kill, and to destroy: I am come that they might have life, and that they might have it more abundantly" (John 10:8-10).

All of us are being controlled either by Jesus or by Satan. If Jesus is not the Master of your life, then whether you realize it or not, Satan is the master of your life. Jesus said, "No man can serve two masters." But it is true that every man does serve one master. Jesus said about the enemy, "He's come to rob, to kill, to destroy. In contrast, I have come that you might have life, and that more abundantly." If your life is mastered by Satan, then he is robbing you of the rich blessings of living in fellowship with God. He is robbing you of the gift of God, which is eternal life through Jesus Christ. He is robbing you of your reasoning capacities. And ultimately, he will rob you of your health and of physical life itself. Jesus said, "He's come to destroy." He destroys your conscience. He will destroy you physically, emotionally, and spiritually. If your life is mastered by Satan, know this: he has come to kill. He will kill all spiritual longing for goodness. He will kill your desire for God. He will kill your power to resist evil. And he will ultimately kill and damn your soul forever.

But in sharp contrast, Jesus said, "But I have come that you might have life, and that more abundantly." The word there for "abundantly" is *perissos* and what it means at its core is excessive. Superabundant. Exceedingly abundant. Beyond measure. When was the last time someone offered you something that good? When was the last time someone cared enough about you that they wanted you to have an excessive amount of anything—unless they attached a lot of strings or financial agreements to that deal? And yet this abundant life, this incredible, unmatchable, unspeakable gift of God is free—totally and completely. It's free to you, although it cost God everything.

We can know the abundant life only through the Christ Child. The Bible tells us this about that Child: He was "meek and lowly in heart" (Matthew 11:29), "a lamb without blemish and without spot" (1 Peter 1:19) who "was in all points tempted as we are, yet without sin" (Hebrews 4:15). That means that He is aware of our temptations and acquainted with all our ways. That means we can come to Him for comfort, direction and strength. The Child in the manger grew to be a Man who would walk to the cross in our place; a Man who would lay His hands willingly against that wood and permit nails to be driven through His flesh, so that we could have a blood covering for our sin. And He would endure three days of death so that we would never need to know the permanence of death, and would rise again that we might have the hope of a resurrection.

The world can't offer you enough toys or trinkets to match that gift. Once you see the real thing, you can never be satisfied with a substitute.

John wrote,

> "And this is the testimony: that God has given us eternal life, and this life is in His Son. He who has the Son has life; he who

does not have the Son of God does not have life" (1 John 5:11-12 NKJV).

Where are you today? Where do you stand? What dark hillside have you been dwelling on? The tidings have come. The message has been given. And now the choice stands before you: "Will you accept God's gift and let Jesus transform your life and give you an abundant, eternal existence, full of hope and joy and peace? Or will you walk away unchanged, empty, without purpose or hope?"

Choose well. Let the glad tidings of God pierce through your darkness and stir your soul. Turn, look at the Child, and let Him come into your heart and change your life eternally.

There in Bethlehem, no room could be found for the Savior. That same tragedy exists today.

Many have filled their lives with distractions, sin, and pleasure that they can't or won't make room for Jesus. But it doesn't have to be that way. You can make a place for Him in your heart. It's as simple as yielding your life and surrendering your will. If you want God's gift, all you have to do is ask. He's listening. Let Him hear your heart. "Jesus, I'm tired of trying to direct my life. I need You. I need Your forgiveness. Please be the Lord of my life. I relinquish the rule of my heart to You. Indwell me and change me."

A line in a popular Christmas movie says, "Every time you hear a bell, it means another angel got its wings." There's no truth to that line. But it is true that every time a lost child prays a prayer of repentance, the angels in heaven celebrate. If you've just prayed that prayer for the first time, know that you've caused a celebration among the heavenly host.

And with that, we come to the end of our story . . . but it's not the end of The Story. May the One who wrote every page of history and who knows the future continue to write His love across your life. May He bless you as you go out in the midst of a world that doesn't understand what Christmas is all about, a world that is pushing and shoving and grabbing and grasping. May the peace of Christ, the love of God, the presence of the Holy Spirit overshadow you and give you strength, keep your mind centered on Him, and help you to live above the darkness of this world.

> Father, we thank You that You so loved the world that You gave us Your only begotten Son, who bore in His own body our sins,

who died in our place, who rose again and ascended into heaven to prepare a place for us, that we might not perish, but that we might be with You in the glorious kingdom of God, world without end.

How can we thank You, Father, for such an unspeakable gift? How can we express our gratitude that You lifted our guilt and shame and bore our sins away? Thank You, Father, for the Babe born in Bethlehem. Thank You for Christmas when we can celebrate that gift. Thank You for the offer of abundant, eternal life. Make us, Lord, very conscious of the purpose of that gift—and teach us to treasure Him.

In Jesus' name we pray.

Amen